# BRUSSELS TYPE

STAN VAN STEENDAM

# BRUSSELS TYPE

LUSTER

*To Dries, who always is a great support.*

Street lettering is something spanning all ages: you can read the continuous change of a city through its street typography. Time and again, façades are plastered and daubed over, making them almost completely invisible. BRUSSELS TYPE is a close-up of a city going through the process of change. It contains snapshots from the streets of Brussels which illustrate the transience of what was once carefully painted, set or carved out. At the same time, BRUSSELS TYPE is also a recording for posterity, a rendering of the atmosphere and aesthetics in Brussels.

I am obsessed by letters. They keep me sharp and alert. I love walking around a bustling city, along broad boulevards, across market squares, through narrow alleys, while being led by letters. Each walk around the city produces a different story. Street typography can be seen everywhere, and mostly in places you least expect. And yet letters often remain invisible to the indifferent passer-by and the unsuspecting tourist. They have been there for decades and have become an integral part of the familiar and transient street scene. All of these letters were once set, painted and carved out, either to attract attention, to lure buyers or to spread a message. Today, they are faded, removed, painted over, pasted over and torn down.

STAN VAN STEENDAM

Luchtvaartsquare, Anderlecht
Square de l'Aviation, Anderlecht

Kroonlaan, Elsene
Avenue de la Couronne, Ixelles

Spaarzaamheidstraat, Brussel
Rue de l'Economie, Bruxelles

Liedtsplein, Schaarbeek
Place Liedts, Schaerbeek

Adolphe Buyllaan, Elsene
Avenue Adolphe Buyl, Ixelles

Steenkoolkaai, Brussel
Quai à la Houille, Bruxelles

Louis Bertrandlaan, Schaarbeek
Avenue Louis Bertrand, Schaerbeek

Groot Eiland, Brussel
Rue de la Grande Ile, Bruxelles

Jourdanstraat, Sint-Gillis
Rue Jourdan, Saint-Gilles

Baksteenkaai, Brussel
Quai aux Briques, Bruxelles

De Merodestraat, Sint-Gillis
Rue de Mérode, Saint-Gilles

Oppemstraat, Brussel
Rue d'Ophem, Bruxelles

Philippe de Champagnestraat, Brussel
Rue Philippe de Champagne, Bruxelles

Roostersteeg, Brussel
Impasse du Gril, Bruxelles

Baksteenkaai, Brussel
Quai aux Briques, Bruxelles

Nijverheidskaai, Anderlecht
Quai de l'Industrie, Anderlecht

Bergensesteenweg, Anderlecht
Chaussée de Mons, Anderlecht

Bergensesteenweg, Anderlecht
Chaussée de Mons, Anderlecht

LES FLEURS DU SPORTING     Tél: 02/521.83.19

Emile Jacqmainlaan, Brussel
Boulevard Emile Jacqmain, Bruxelles

Anderlechtsesteenweg, Brussel
Rue d'Anderlecht, Bruxelles

Blaesstraat, Brussel
Rue Blaes, Bruxelles

Kiekenmarkt, Brussel
Rue du Marché aux Poulets, Bruxelles

Kartuizerstraat, Brussel
Rue des Chartreux, Bruxelles

Blaesstraat, Brussel
Rue Blaes, Bruxelles

Coenraetsstraat, Sint-Gillis
Rue Coenraets, Saint-Gilles

Antwerpsesteenweg, Brussel
Chaussée d'Anvers, Bruxelles

Hoogstraat, Brussel
Rue Haute, Bruxelles

Huidevettersstraat, Brussel
Rue des Tanneurs, Bruxelles

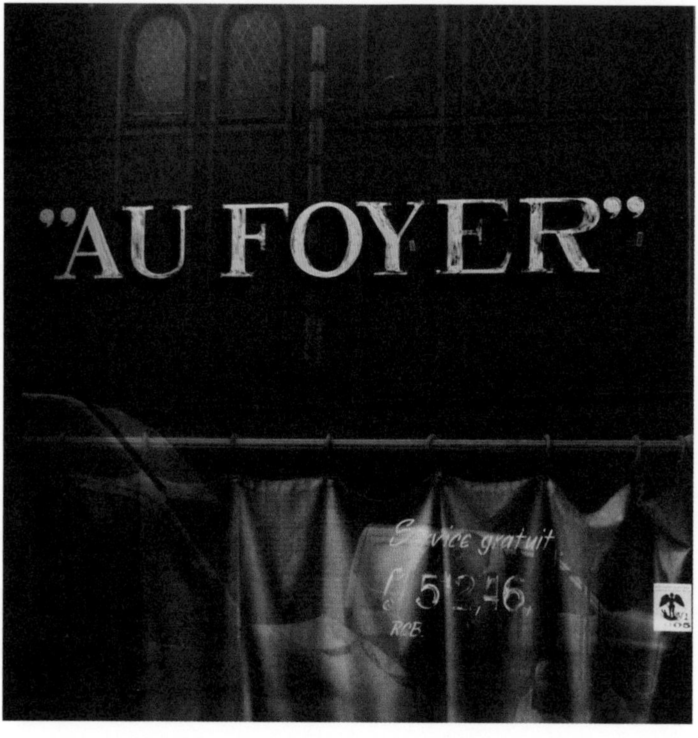
"AU FOYER"
vice gratuit
RCB.

Ruslandstraat, Sint-Gillis
Rue de Russie, Saint-Gilles

Sint-Gilliskerkstraat, Sint-Gillis
Rue de l'Eglise Saint-Gilles, Saint-Gilles

Vossenplein, Brussel
Place du Jeu de Balle, Bruxelles

Jean Volderslaan, Sint-Gillis
Avenue Jean Volders, Saint-Gilles

Steenweg op Ninove, Anderlecht
Chaussée de Ninove, Anderlecht

Keienveldstraat, Elsene
Rue Keyenveld, Ixelles

Bergensesteenweg, Anderlecht
Chaussée de Mons, Anderlecht

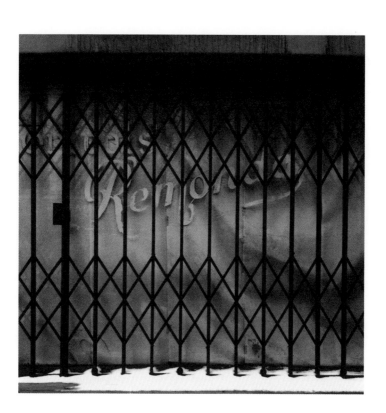

Koninglaan, Vorst
Avenue du Roi, Forest

Joseph Claesstraat, Sint-Gillis
Rue Joseph Claes, Saint-Gilles

Reebokstraat, Brussel
Rue du Chevreuil, Bruxelles

MAISON COOREMAN
VOLAILLE GIBIER
WILD en GEVOGELTE Gros-Détail
Poulets à la Broche
chez Mariatje

Anneessensstraat, Brussel
Rue Anneessens, Bruxelles

Koopliedenstraat, Brussel
Rue des Commerçants, Bruxelles

Stalingradlaan, Brussel
Avenue de Stalingrad, Bruxelles

Hoogstraat, Brussel
Rue Haute, Bruxelles

Gallaitstraat, Schaarbeek
Rue Gallait, Schaerbeek

Vaartstraat, Brussel
Rue du Canal, Bruxelles

Papenvest, Brussel
Rue du Rempart de Moines, Bruxelles

Sleutelstraat, Brussel
Rue de la Clé, Bruxelles

Sint Goriksplein, Brussel
Place Saint-Géry, Bruxelles

Dieudonné Lefèvrestraat, Laken
Rue Dieudonné Lefèvre, Laeken

Arteveldestraat, Brussel
Rue Van Artevelde, Bruxelles

Argonnestraat, Sint-Gillis
Rue de l'Argonne, Saint-Gilles

Blaesstraat, Brussel
Rue Blaes, Bruxelles

Paalstraat, Sint-Jans-Molenbeek
Rue de la Colonne, Molenbeek-Saint-Jean

Koninginnegalerij, Brussel
Galerie de la Reine, Bruxelles

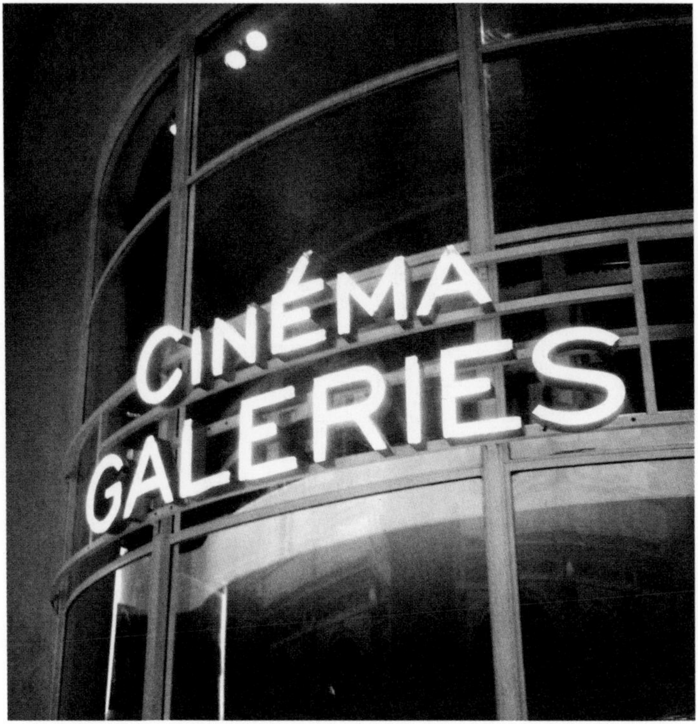
CINÉMA
GALERIES

Louis Hapstraat, Etterbeek
Rue Louis Hap, Etterbeek

Romestraat, Sint-Gillis
Rue de Rome, Saint-Gilles

Romestraat, Sint-Gillis
Rue de Rome, Saint-Gilles

Kolenmarkt, Brussel
Rue du Marché au Charbon, Bruxelles

Anspachlaan, Brussel
Boulevard Anspach, Bruxelles

Koninginnelaan, Laken
Avenue de la Reine, Laeken

Edmond Bonehillstraat, Sint-Jans-Molenbeek
Rue Edmond Bonehill, Molenbeek-Saint-Jean

Oudergemlaan, Etterbeek
Avenue d'Auderghem, Etterbeek

Louis Hapstraat, Etterbeek
Rue Louis Hap, Etterbeek

Minimenstraat, Brussel
Rue des Minimes, Bruxelles

Moutstraat, Brussel
Rue de la Braie, Bruxelles

Philippe Baucqstraat, Etterbeek
Rue Philippe Baucq, Etterbeek

Spoormakersstraat, Brussel
Rue des Eperonniers, Bruxelles

Spoormakersstraat, Brussel
Rue des Eperonniers, Bruxelles

Stoofstraat, Brussel
Rue de l'Etuve, Bruxelles

Vier-windenstraat, Sint-Jans-Molenbeek
Rue des Quatre-Vents, Molenbeek-Saint-Jean

Taborastraat, Brussel
Rue de Tabora, Bruxelles

Grasmarkt, Brussel
Rue du Marché aux Herbes, Bruxelles

Voldersstraat, Brussel
Rue des Foulons, Bruxelles

Fortstraat, Sint-Gillis
Rue du Fort, Saint-Gilles

Boucherie
BOUCHERIE ISLADELICE مجزرة الإسلامية
Agneau-Boeuf-Veau-Poulet
Merguez-Brochette-Pitta

Circusstraat, Brussel
Rue du Cirque, Bruxelles

Lakensestraat, Brussel
Rue de Laeken, Bruxelles

Arteveldestraat, Brussel
Rue Van Artevelde, Bruxelles

Zuidlaan, Brussel
Boulevard du Midi, Bruxelles

Steenweg op Gent, Sint-Jans-Molenbeek
Chaussée de Gand, Molenbeek-Saint-Jean

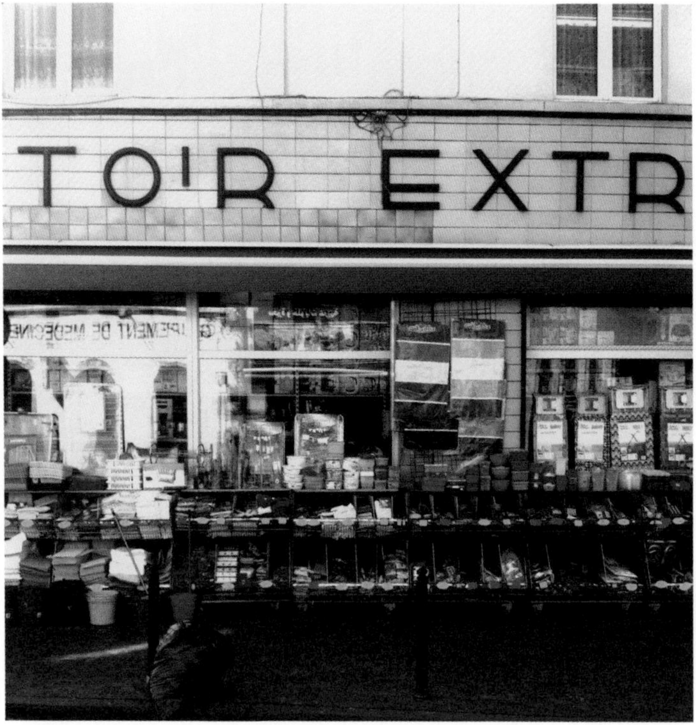
TOIR EXTR

●

Schoolstraat, Sint-Jans-Molenbeek
Rue de l'Ecole, Molenbeek-Saint-Jean

Sint-Katelijnestraat, Brussel
Rue Sainte-Catherine, Bruxelles

Brussels Type

Photography and Typographic Design: Stan Van Steendam

D/2013/12.005/5
ISBN 978 94 6058 1168
NUR 656
copyright 2013 Luster, Antwerp
www.lusterweb.com
Printed in Belgium